CONSTRUCTIVE
COMMUNICATION

A PATH FOR CHALLENGING SITUATIONS

CHARLIE YOUNG

Suite 300 - 990 Fort St
Victoria, BC, v8v 3K2
Canada

www.friesenpress.com

Copyright © 2017 by Charlie Young
First Edition — 2017

charlie.y.bend@gmail.com

All rights reserved.

No part of this publication may be reproduced in any form, or by any means, electronic or mechanical, including photocopying, recording, or any information browsing, storage, or retrieval system, without permission in writing from FriesenPress.

ISBN
978-1-5255-1602-3 (Hardcover)
978-1-5255-1603-0 (Paperback)
978-1-5255-1604-7 (eBook)

1. FAMILY & RELATIONSHIPS, CONFLICT RESOLUTION

Distributed to the trade by The Ingram Book Company

TABLE OF CONTENTS

ix	INTRODUCTION
xiii	PART ONE
1	PERCEPTIONS
7	COMMUNICATION HINDRANCES
11	BASIC COMMUNICATION BEHAVIORS
17	COMMUNICATION TOOLS
21	EMOTIONS
27	INCLUSIVE COMMUNICATION
35	HELPS FOR RESOLUTION
41	THE BLOCK GAME
45	VISUALS
47	PART TWO
49	THE PATH FOR CHALLENGING SITUATIONS
53	THE OPENING STATEMENT
59	STORY TELLING
65	UNDERSTANDING
69	BRAINSTORMING
75	SOLUTIONS
83	ABOUT THE AUTHOR
85	SOURCES THAT HAVE INFLUENCED THE CONCEPTS OF THIS BOOK

"Educating the mind without educating the heart is no education at all."

—Aristotle

Dedicated to
Donna, my wife.

Without her support, editing, suggestions and direction,
this guide would not have happened.

INTRODUCTION

This guide is intended for those who wish to develop effective communication skills. Its goal is to assist communicating for common understandings, better relationships and trust. Common understanding does not necessarily indicate agreement. The guide is written to be easily understood and practical. It avoids technicalities. These can be explored in more depth by entering key words on a search engine. Constructive communication is inclusive. In this guide the two terms - constructive and inclusive - are used interchangeably. It's all about having meaningful conversations.

Each chapter of the first part of this guide has a basic concept. Make it your own. Flesh it out with your own concepts. Like a guide to a foreign country, each chapter gets you to a location, but you need to experience it and bring back memories to share. The essence of a good guide is to get you there. Once arrived at, the experience is what you make of it.

The second part provides a mentored path for challenging situations. Normally you won't need it. This mentored path provides a means to apply the principles of inclusive communication when dialogue is a challenge. The path is applicable for all types of difficult situations.

The principles of inclusive communication apply in normal and challenging communications.

My suggestions are specific and will be updated and improved as those who use this guide share their experiences with me.

Duplication of the contents of this guide is with the permission of the author. This assures that the reader has the latest material and protects the value of the hours spent in the guide's creation.

Learning means that a behavioral change has taken place. We may know something, but we haven't learned it until there has been a behavioral change. The paradigms of our patterns of speech and conversation are often difficult to change. Application and practice of the concepts about to be shared are important and will bring about behavioral change and personal growth.

This guide applies to community building, diplomacy, family, businesses and friendships. It's not about the language of military commands, air traffic control, court proceedings, surgical procedures etc.

There are visual aids for those who find them helpful.

In changing communication paradigms remember that 90+% of communication is non-verbal. If your communication is not in synch with your self-image, concepts and interests, it will be seen as bogus. When all is in synch, the non-verbal takes care of itself.

Conflict presents opportunities to grow. The history of man reflects that the great advances in science and the humanities grew out of questioning, disagreement and finally resolution. Inclusive communication generates progress from diversity.

Note that he is used rather than alternating between he or she. This simplified the text and made the thoughts flow more easily.

> *"It is the mark of an educated man to be able to entertain a thought without accepting it."*
>
> —Aristotle

CONSTRUCTIVE COMMUNICATION

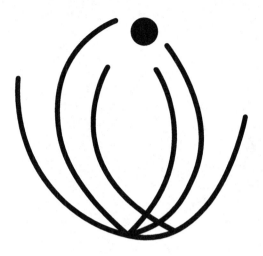

The seed of understanding

The seed symbolizes that once understanding emerges the blessings of growth result.

PART ONE

CHAPTER ONE

PERCEPTIONS

Perceptions are the ways people perceive, (see, hear, feel, smell and understand things). The same thing can be perceived in different ways by different people. This is a difficult concept.

When we're talking with people and trying to come to a common understanding, we do it through the lenses of our own experiences. They do it through the lenses of their experiences. Conflict or misunderstanding can change into an opportunity by seeing something from a different point of view. We simply need to be open to another viewpoint. This guide concentrates on the tools needed for this to happen.

If you have difficulty with the concept of people having different perceptions about the same experience, fact, teaching, colors, etc. please reflect on this. Failure to accept this concept, presents a barrier to behavioral change in our communication style and is a hindrance to empathy.

Let's take a few simple examples.

Take a mixing bowl and ask, while looking at it from above, if it is convex or concave. Now turn it over and ask the same question. It all depends on your perspective.

For us, poor people in a third world country have no running water, live hand to mouth, have little or no medical care and their homes are of cardboard with a corrugated steel roof. Now we speak of the poor people in our country as having running hot and cold water, nourishing food, medical care, and a home with heating and a shingled roof.

Our perspective on poverty changes dramatically as our experience changes. For people in the third world, our poor are well off. The perspective of the poor in our country is that they lack amenities most people have.

Parents walk into a jail where their child is being held for theft. The child perceives anger, but the parents are frustrated. They wonder where they failed at teaching honesty. Absolutely different perceptions.

A student questions a teacher about the thinking behind a mathematical formula. The student is truly interested because he wishes to be an engineer. The teacher perceives a challenge to his authority.

Parents have serious differences regarding the problems their child is having. One parent perceives laziness. The other perceives a medical or other problem.

Look at the two following drawings. The first can be seen as a cup or two people looking at each other. It depends on our focus. The second drawing can be seen as a young woman or an older one. Again it depends on where we put our focus. Transfer these thoughts to trying to understand the thoughts of another. Our perceptions of their thinking result from our past experience and where we put our emphasis.

The following are examples of different perceptions. You can certainly multiply these from your own experiences. Our task is to accept these differences and develop communication skills to reach common understanding.

The point is that we all see, hear, smell, feel and emotionally comprehend things from our perspective through the lenses of our experience. So what might smell bad to us might smell good to another person. Fear might be part of this experience which is the basis for many of our emotions. Past experiences might, without our knowing it, be having an effect on us.

CONSTRUCTIVE COMMUNICATION

We might have a fear of heights whereas others are very comfortable working hundreds of feet above the ground. Constantly seeing violence on TV and movies for the resolution of differences may form our perceptions on how to resolve differences.

Another analogy is that of a doe with two fawns. One ends up at a farm and gets imprinted on the people there. The other lives in the forest with her mom. Thus, one fawn, from experience, has no fear of people and the other is full of fear of people. Now think of children raised in dysfunctional families and children raised in loving empathetic families.

When I was attending a Spanish class in Mexico City a man who seemed opinionated argued at length with the professor on the proper pronunciation of teléfono. The accent is on the second e and the student insisted it was on the next to last o. He was arguing with a Mexican professor whose native language was Spanish on how to pronounce a Spanish word. It was ludicrous, but taught me how imbedded people's perceptions can be.

While conversing with others, keep in mind the different perceptions people have due to their experiences. What I am saying might be interpreted in a different way by the listener.

Understanding the concept of perceptions assists in applying the tools that follow.

OUR MOST IMPORTANT PERCEPTION

Our most important perception is the one we have of ourselves. This affects all our communications with others. Most people refer to this as our self-image. This may not be who we are deep inside. Our self-image may be blocking our real self from showing. Many people, because of past experiences, have trouble showing their true self. Inclusive communication with the right people and/or possibly counseling or spiritual direction helps our self-image develop and our lives change for the better.

If we don't challenge this perception (our self-image) then we will tend to accommodate new ideas to fit this perception rather than questioning these new ideas.

The perception of ourselves and the perceptions of our conversations affect understandings.

DIFFERENT PERCEPTIONS OF THE SAME THING

For some:

- A hike of five or six miles is long. For others it's normal.
- Getting home after 9:00 pm is late. For others this is normal.
- Helping others is a joy for some. Others find it difficult.
- Being number one is the most important thing for some. For others, being number one is secondary to working together as equals.

"Experience is the teacher of all things."

—Julius Caesar

CHAPTER TWO

COMMUNICATION HINDRANCES

What are some hindrances to good communication? Not willing to talk, afraid, angry, don't know the answer, get out of my face, etc. Addressing these challenges is covered in the following four chapters.

There are three main hindrances to good communication.

1. Lack of good faith
2. Lack of trust
3. Inability to communicate clearly

LACK OF GOOD FAITH

Good faith is the openness and desire to understand the other person. It is the foundation of all good communication. It permeates inclusive communication. Lying is contrary to good faith.

During a mediation I simply explain good faith in the following way. I tell the participants that, "When the other person is talking don't try to figure out how to answer him." I emphasize this by repeating, "Do NOT try to figure out how to answer him. Try to figure out what he is saying." I'm stressing one of the skills of inclusive communication.

Without this good faith of wanting to hear and understand the other side, chances of resolution are greatly diminished. A person needs to know that we're trying to understand his perceptions.

A good example of a lack of good faith is using "you" statements in lieu of "I" statements. By pointing a finger at a person while saying **"you"** with emphasis, we're sending a message of I already know your perception. For example, "You don't have the facts straight." As opposed to "I don't think you have the facts straight." We can soften the "you" with "I think that you," or something similar. This puts the responsibility of the perception on me rather than the other person. Another good example is physically pushing a person. The natural reaction is to push back. It's the same with emphasizing "you" without the softening of "I think" or another softening phrase.

LACK OF TRUST

Trust is putting our confidence in another person and accepting him into our personal world. It's saying to ourselves that this person has integrity. He is who he says and appears to be.

Trust is lost by a lie, lack of dependability, failure to do an assigned task etc.

Trust is important so that we can depend on someone and share with them without the worry of personal things being blabbered.

Lost trust is hard to get back. The best way to restore trust is by small steps rather than a leap. If we make a leap we fall way back if we falter. If we take small steps the falter results in less loss of trust. Small steps create a better process for creating a lasting trust. Small steps take longer but usually result in strengthening a trust relationship over the long term.

A good way to start to regain trust is to simply ask, "What do I need to do to gain or regain your trust?" This simple sentence sends many messages, but it is sure hard to say.

INABILITY TO COMMUNICATE CLEARLY

People don't communicate clearly because they're scared to say what they think, have not been taught how to speak clearly or are afraid they won't say it correctly. Some people for various reasons do not communicate clearly, concisely and consistently.

A good way to address the issue of the inability to communicate clearly is to emphasize paraphrasing and open ended questions.

SUMMARY

Removing the above obstacles will help us to communicate better. We need to choose the best method for us to accomplish this.

> It's easier to communicate well when there's a feeling of good faith and trust. The rest of the guide is dedicated to developing skills for communicating clearly.

"If your actions inspire others to dream more, learn more, do more and become more, you are a leader."

—John Quincy Adams

CHAPTER THREE

BASIC COMMUNICATION BEHAVIORS

We've covered a few ideas about good communication. Now we'll cover some behaviors that help communication. Later we'll refer to some tools for communication. Behaviors help us develop a style of communication.

Mediators employ the following behavioral skills in assisting parties to mutual understandings. These behaviors are usually referred to with the acronym **VECS**. They work. These behaviors energize the communication tools that are covered later in this guide.

VECS stands for:

- **V**alidate
- **E**mpathize
- **C**larify
- **S**ummarize

VECS refers to behaviors we project toward other people when we're talking with them. Ideally they project VECS back to us which initiates communication toward common understandings.

VALIDATE

I'm going to talk with each person in such a way that he knows that I consider what he says is important to him. It's a way of showing respect. Notice, I didn't say that it may be important to me. Validating addresses facts. If we don't validate, the other person may pick up the message that I consider him unimportant because I don't care about his interests. Validating is significant in creating understandings, relationships and trust.

A point of interest: If we or our ideas have not been regularly validated, we'll probably have difficulty validating others and their ideas. Our perceptions, including how we say things, normally come from our experiences.

**The following examples demonstrate validating.
The fact, my perception, is underlined.**

"Hank, your <u>idea</u> on how to build the bridge might save us a great deal of money. It's worth our time to talk about it."

"Mary, that new afghan of yours is <u>beautiful</u>. I love the design and colors you picked out for it. It took a great deal of <u>work</u>."

"There aren't many people who could have <u>figured that out</u> as well as you did."

"With some practice and effort your <u>writing talents</u> could really turn into something."

EMPATHIZE

Empathy is an important tool for good communication. It's linked with understanding perceptions. Empathy addresses emotions, which establishes a core response mode of a person. Empathy is NOT sympathy. It lets the person know that we're trying to understand how he feels. One element of empathy is simply our presence. This is why people often hug during emotional times. You're identifying with where the person is emotionally at the present moment. Once established, empathy opens the door to sharing. Following are some examples and two definitions.

Examples of Empathy
The emotion is underlined.

1. That must have been really difficult and <u>worrisome</u> for you.

2. Wow! That must have been <u>fun</u>.

3. That must have <u>upset</u> you.

4. Your loss must have been <u>painful</u>.

Empathy is the experience of understanding another person's condition from his perspective. Note: This isn't intellectual. It's about emotions.

Empathy is the ability to understand another's emotional perspective and to consider it before acting.

There are levels of empathy. The deeper the level of empathy, the more the openness to common understanding. Psychological research confirms this.

- Cognitive empathy – we recognize what a person is feeling.
- Emotional empathy – we actually feel what the person is feeling. Research shows that this is particularly true when we have experienced what is causing the feelings of the other person.
- Compassionate empathy – we want to help the person deal with his situation and emotions.

Here are a few ways that will improve our tendencies to be empathetic.

- Expanding our human experiences
- Developing our humanity through meditation, spiritual exercises, counseling, etc.
- Reading books that allow us to project ourselves into filling out the characters' emotional reactions to situations
- Accepting that emotions arise from perceptions.

In the following example the empathy parts are bold. Read with and without the empathy parts to experience the difference.

"Hi John, I was sorry to hear about your car accident. **You must feel upset like I did when my car was T boned.** Let me know if there's anything I can do."

"Anne, I had the same surgery and doctor. **It must have been difficult to decide to go ahead with it. I know it was for me. Now that it's over you must be happy over its success.** Let's celebrate and go out to dinner together."

"Wow! I never scored that well in any of the tests I've taken. **What a good feeling you must have for acing the test.**"

A simple way I have of referring to empathy is that it is really about being human. It's living in the present while being discerning as to specifics but not judgmental of people. We empathize with people's emotions no matter their cause.

An analogy for empathy that has been meaningful to me is to think of walking in their shoes. Reflecting on this, I find it harder to get out of my own shoes first, and certainly I can't walk in the other person's shoes until I get out of mine.

To practice empathy our whole being needs to be engaged. It's easier if we acknowledge the different perceptions people have of the same subject.

> In tough situations empathy is often the ice breaker

CLARIFY

Clarifying here is not a tool, but an attitude or behavior (courteous curiosity) that establishes that we really want to understand what the other person is saying. Clarifying will be explained later in the guide as a tool.

From my experience, when I clarify what I think the other person has said, they often clarify my words. This clarification of a clarification establishes a relational dialogue. It reflects a comfort level of feeling free to assure understanding.

The following is an example of clarifying as a behavior.

"John, I think the reason the plane crashed was that it stalled. The pilot didn't recover from the spin, and the plane went into the ground."

"You mean that the engine gave up the ghost and without power the plane just fell out of the sky? That's what it looked like on the evening news."

"No, John. What I meant to say is that because the way the plane was flown, its wings lost lift and without lift it couldn't fly. When it lost its lift, rather than the pilot recovering, he probably misused the controls and the plane nosed down and started spinning down until it crashed."

"You mean that most likely the engine was still running properly."

"Yes, that's exactly what I meant. It was a question of loss of lift."

Both parties had a courteous curiosity and entered into a meaningful conversation that clarified a misunderstanding.

SUMMARIZE

Summarizing is taking the ideas a person has shared with me and saying them back in an abbreviated form.

As a behavior it lets the other person know that I understand and that I'm interested.

The following is an example of a summary of another person's explanation of a concept.

"My understanding of what you said is that my car insurance will cover my wife and me as drivers and anyone else over 21. If someone under

21 is driving my car alone and has an accident the insurance doesn't cover this, but I can have my children with driver's permits drive the car while I'm supervising from the passenger's seat and the insurance is in force."

This is often followed by a clarification.

"You understand most of my explanation, but you forgot to mention that the coverage for your children under your supervision is only valid in this state. It's a little thing, but important."

> *"I do not ask the wounded person how he feels,*
> *I myself become the wounded person."*
>
> —Walt Whitman

CHAPTER FOUR

COMMUNICATION TOOLS

SPECIFIC TOOLS FOR COMMUNICATING WELL

- Paraphrasing
- Open ended questions
- Clarifying
- Repeating exactly what you heard

These tools assist reaching common understanding. We say that we understand why a person holds a certain position, even though we may not agree with it. Without common understanding there is little hope for developing relationships, better communities or happy families. Though I may disagree, I now understand why we disagree, and can live with it or develop a compromise which suits all parties.

The parties now feel they understand and they feel understood.

PARAPHRASING

Paraphrasing is saying back in our own words our understanding of the perception of the other person. Frequently, from my experience, when I paraphrase the other person will say, "That's not exactly what I meant." Paraphrasing is important. Failure to paraphrase lacks the reaffirmation of understanding the other person's perception.

CLARIFYING

Clarifying assures that we understand what the other person means by asking questions, giving examples etc. We're affirming that we want the perception of the other person to be clear in our mind. Analogies are sometimes helpful.

OPEN ENDED QUESTIONS

An open ended question is one that can't be answered with yes or no. Its intent is to get the person to reply with an explanation rather than with a yes or no answer. For example: "Would you explain why you feel John is not carrying his share of the load?" A valuable open ended question is why. It can lead to the interests behind a position and open a discussion regarding the reasons for a particular conviction.

REPEATING EXACTLY WHAT WE HEARD

This is simply repeating what we heard in the same words. Repeating exactly what we heard does not guarantee that we understand what we heard.

Repeating needs to carry a message of honest curiosity.

Example – The area of a circle is equal to pi times the radius squared or $a=\pi r^2$. Personally, I can say this but don't ask me to explain why it is so.

THE DYNAMICS OF THE COMMUNICATION TOOLS

   It creates a bond between the parties by:
- Sending a message of wanting to understand
- Accepting your ideas as important and thus you are important
- Wanting to understand each other
- Desiring to feel understood
- This process evolves into more and more sharing.

CONSTRUCTIVE COMMUNICATION

> *"Kind words do not cost much.*
> *Yet they accomplish much."*
>
> —Blaise Pascal

CHAPTER FIVE
EMOTIONS

We all have feelings and emotions. They are part of the human condition. To deny them is to deny part of our humanity. We have to learn to use them constructively. We get angry, fearful, happy, sorrowful, euphoric, down, up, scared, frustrated, etc.

Emotions are part of being human. They are part of communication. They can hinder inclusive communication or can help it. They are part of the 90+% of non-verbal communication.

Emotions affect our communication, and unless specifically identified, they can be misinterpreted and we won't know what need is behind the emotion. For example, frustration is often interpreted as anger. Thus, I might need to say, "I'm not angry. I'm frustrated because I don't understand why you did this." But the listener may still perceives anger, and I may have to reassure him several times.

To communicate well we need to identify the emotion(s) we are experiencing. Emotions of themselves are neutral. Often we don't even know what caused them. It could be something in our past, a word, a sound, a smell, a photo, a body posture etc. An emotion of itself is neutral.

What we do with our emotions and how we handle them is important. By identifying them and the needs or expectations that they reflect, we can learn to control them and use them to improve our communication. Expectations are often wants which, though not necessary, can be the force behind our emotions.

Emotions tend to overpower when we deny their presence. Emotions constrict our openness to other's perceptions and can narrow our vision to hazards. I had a student pilot who was fearful of making a mistake and wanted everything perfect. He got so engrossed in his fears and desires, he wasn't relaxed enough to see a plane heading right toward us for a possible mid-air collision. This often happens in communication when emotions take over.

By acknowledging the presence of an emotion, we are on the path to handling it through identifying the need or expectation behind it. We can then decide how to use it properly. Emotions need to be used constructively not destructively. I refer to people who project negative perceptions such as anger, self-pity, feeling helpless etc. as carrying a monkey on their back. They need to get rid of the monkey and become constructive through positive emotions such as joy, hope etc. With the monkey gone people start to grow and live. To get rid of the monkey they need to accept that it's there.

- Frustrated people lose the openness to creative thought.
- Fearful people often have their thinking and even peripheral vision contract.
- People in a downer hesitate to experiment or question.
- Euphoric people are usually open to change and new experiences.
- Anger can so affect a person's communication that he makes no sense.

Communication can be faulty if we don't identify the emotions that come from our needs or expectations. Once identified we can start to handle our emotions properly. Strong emotions can fog or even black out our reasoning. The table at the end of this chapter identifies the needs behind emotions.

CONSTRUCTIVE COMMUNICATION

THE FOLLOWING DIAGRAM ON THE CONTINUUM OF THOUGHT, EMOTION, DECISION AND CONSEQUENCES IS BUILT AROUND A SQUARE TO TRY TO EMPHASIZE THAT THERE ARE CRITICAL COMMUNICATION POINTS WHICH ARE GOOD TO IDENTIFY. THERE IS ANOTHER MORE FLOWING DIAGRAM AT THE END OF PART ONE.

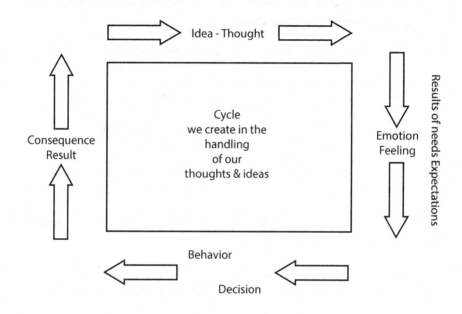

<u>Either Constructive or Destructive</u>
The decision to be constructive should address needs and expectations.

Expressing our needs or expectations provides a path to common understanding, trust and relationships. To do this, we have to identify our needs or expectations while remembering that the other person also has needs and expectations.

**Needs or expectations need to be verbalized.
The following are some examples.**

- "Dad, I want to feel comfortable trying to assemble this computer knowing that I might fail." (**need to be trusted**)
- "Mom, I would like to feel part of the planning for John's birthday party." (**need** to be **accepted**)
- "I hope you (a teacher) realize my struggle with math. I need to feel that you understand." (**need to be understood**)
- "John, I also need to feel understood." (**need to be accepted**)
- "Bob (a friend) I want to feel good about us working out this problem together." (**need to be accepted**)
- "I feel hopeful because you're listening to my side of the story." (**need closeness**)
- "Dad, I feel good that you let me use the car for the prom." (**need to be trusted**)
- "Class, I sense something good coming out of our working together for the homeless shelter." (**need a dream to come true**)

Develop some other scenarios from your own experience. We need to get used to trying to identify our needs or expectations because they're behind our emotions.

There is a connection between emotions and empathy. People like to know that we're trying to understand how they feel, and we need to show empathy toward ourselves. It's nice to have a friend who understands how I feel. It's even nicer to know how and why I feel this way.

Empathizing identifies with the other person's emotions. It helps them identify these emotions and then deal with them. Good communication is difficult when clouded with obstructing emotions.

Only we can change what we do with our feelings.

CONSTRUCTIVE COMMUNICATION

> *"Understand the enemy and you can defeat him.*
> *Understand yourself and there is no enemy."*
>
> —Ancient Chinese Proverb

The following table shows some relationships between feelings and needs. Note the different feelings that arise when needs are met and when they are not met.

This table made available from PuddleDancer Press and the Center for Nonviolent Communication

FEELINGS AND NEEDS from Nonviolent Communication
by Marshall B. Rosenberg

Feelings when needs "are" fulfilled

Amazed	Joyous	Comfortable	Moved
Confident	Optimistic	Eager	Proud
Energetic	Relieved	Fulfilled	Stimulated
Glad	Surprised	Hopeful	Thankful
Inspired	Touched	Intrigued	Trustful

Feelings when needs "are not" fulfilled

Angry	Hopeless	Annoyed	Impatient
Confused	Irritated	Concerned	Lonely
Disappointed	Nervous	Discouraged	Overwhelmed
Distressed	Puzzled	Embarrassed	Reluctant
Frustrated	Sad	Helpless	Uncomfortable

Some Basic Needs We All Have

Autonomy	Physical Nurturance
Choosing dreams/goals/values	Air, Food, Water
Choosing plans for fulfilling	Protection from life-threatening forms of life: viruses, bacteria, insects, predatory animals

dreams, goals & values   Movement exercise
                                  Rest, Sexual expression Shelter Touch

Celebration		**Play**	
Celebrate the creation of life		Fun	
and dreams fulfilled.		Laughter	
Celebrate loved ones, etc.			
Integrity		**Spiritual Communion**	
Authenticity	Creativity	Beauty	Harmony
Meaning	Self-worth	Inspiration	Order
		Peace	
Interdependence			
Acceptance	Appreciation	Honesty (the empowering honesty	
Closeness	Community	that enables us to learn from	
		our limitations)	
Consideration			
Contribute to the	Love	Reassurance	
enrichment of life	Respect	Support	
Emotional Safety	Empathy	Trust	Understanding

©2005 by Puddle Dancer Press
www.nonviolentcommuication.com and www.cnvc.org

CHAPTER SIX

INCLUSIVE COMMUNICATION

Inclusive communication combines our communication behavioral styles and tools in a stable way. It includes the concepts of all of the participants. The concept of inclusive communication refers to the overall tenor of a conversation. Inclusive communication reflects our humanness by including concepts with the reasons behind them and their attached emotions. Inclusiveness provides the opportunity for sharing our concepts. It creates receptivity within communication. This receptivity encourages others to understand our concepts while assuring them that we are trying to understand their concepts. Receptivity and inclusiveness usually results in common understandings and trust. When all parties are communicating in an inclusive way communication becomes truly constructive. To the extent that the conversation is not inclusive it is exclusive.

Think of each component: **C**oncept, **Fe**elings, **I**nterests and **H**umanness as being part of a circle. With any one of the components missing the circle becomes cracked, broken or out of shape. It loses its symmetry, i.e., its humanness. Our communication becomes exclusive.

THE CIRCLE OF INCLUSIVE COMMUNICATION

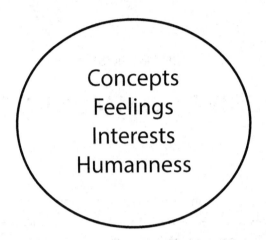

A Concept/Idea/Statement/Observation alone is like a pebble thrown into a pond that sends out emotionless ripples expecting no response.

Feelings or Emotions alone, dump on people. There is nothing to which to respond.

Interests alone create a vacuum. They express why without a concept.

Humanness or Reaching Out alone is mush. A person reaches out but offers nothing.

All four - **C**oncepts, **F**eelings, **I**nterests and **H**umanness - are essential components for inclusive symmetrical communication.

Thoughts on inclusive communication.

> We need:
- to share our concepts and hear the other person's concepts.
- to be open about our feelings and emotions.
- to explain the whys of our concepts. These are our interests.
- to be human and reach out to the other person and provide openings for input.

A non-evaluative/non-judgmental (simply observational) style of communication becomes more creative and open rather than challenging. The listener feels included and more receptive. We're not challenging his needs but trying to meet them. Not separating observation from evaluation threatens open communication, i.e., a true dialogue. Remember the 90+% non-verbal rule. A strong evaluative message can be sent by the tone, loudness or pace of my words or simply by body language. The non-verbal has to be in synch in inclusive communication in order to create open dialogue.

Looking at inclusive communication from a different point of view, words are windows when they come from the heart and are walls when they are heartless. I prefer windows. They let the light in.

We're not saying that every few sentences have to be inclusive, but the overall tenor of the conversation needs to be inclusive.

Because the concept of inclusive communication is so important and pulls together the earlier concepts of communication, behavioral styles and tools, I'm going to give a few examples. I'll note the **(Concepts), (Feelings), (Interests) and (Humanness).** Read each paragraph and then drop out one of the **Concepts, Feelings, Interests or Humanness** and note the difference in the message. The following examples may seem awkward. Sentences miss the non-verbal such as rolling eyes, shuffling feet etc. Try changing the following to fit your style of speaking.

We are changing paradigms. It's not easy.

EXAMPLES

The championship game is tied with one second to go and the star on your team takes a shot which swishes through the basket as the buzzer goes off. Your friend, Says, "Great shot!" **(Concept)** He stands up hollering ecstatically, "We won! We won!" **(Feelings & Interests)** "Wasn't that a great finish for us? **(Humanness)**

Your son comes home from school with the news that he has been chosen to represent the school at the upcoming civics experience at the state capital. You say, "John, I'm really proud of you." **(Concept)** "This makes me happy." **(Feelings & Interests)** "This took a lot of work and commitment." **(Humanness)**

You're inspecting a job site to assure everyone is working safely, and you come upon an employee who is using a tool unsafely. (Your perception) You wait until he's done so you don't surprise him and say, "Bob, I think there is a safer way to use that tool." **(Humanness & Concept)** "I would like to share it with you" **(Feelings & Interests).** "Would you be interested in discussing it with me?" **(Humanness)**

Your best friend has been told that her daughter was killed in an automobile accident. You go over to express your condolences and say, "Helen, I wish I could express how much I feel for your loss. **(Concept & Interest)** I lost my son in the same way and am still experiencing the pain." **(Feelings)** "If there is anything I can do, please let me know." **(Humanness)**

Your husband calls you on the phone and says that he has been in a bad car accident. You say, "Are you okay?" **(Humanness).** "Boy am I glad that you're okay." **(Concept, Feelings & Interest)** "You must be shook up." **(Interest)** "What would you like me to do?" **(Humanness)**

Your daughter has just been told that she didn't make the softball team. You say, "I'm really proud that you tried and feel sorry for you, because you didn't make the cut." **(Concept & Feelings)** "What do you think we can do to improve your chances of making the team next year? **(Humanness & Interests)**

The following is based on an actual case. Details have been changed to maintain confidentiality. This example has both parties eventually practicing inclusive communication. This is the ideal. You may find the ending difficult to believe, but that's what happened.

I'm using it to illustrate what good inclusive communication can accomplish.

Background: The locale is in a housing development in the mountains of NE Montana. The homes are large and set on 5+ acre lots. The property lines are often not well delineated. Home owners can easily walk between homes and not know on whose property they might be walking. The residents like the informal park like setting and the Home Owners' Association rules that promote the natural look.

Setting: An elderly couple had lived there many years. They considered themselves old timers who felt very comfortable and secure in this natural setting. They could just see their neighbor's house through the landscape. It was at least 500 feet from their home. In the neighboring house lived a couple with two sons, 5 and 6 years old. They were renting the home and had moved in about a month ago.

Characters: Anne – elderly lady a longtime resident and Bob – her husband

Chris – the mother of the two small boys ages 5 & 6 and Don – her husband

Story: One beautiful spring day the two boys asked their mom if they could go out and play in the backyard. Mom gave them permission as long as they didn't go too far and kept in sight. She watched them go out a ways and start playing in the dirt and building a fort out of rocks. They were having a great time enjoying themselves and running wild with their imaginations. Chris was enjoying every minute of seeing her sons enjoy the day and the outdoors.

Meanwhile Anne, the elderly woman in the neighboring house, saw the children and came out screaming at the kids to stop moving the rocks around, and stepping on the plants. She told them to go home. Chris saw all of this unfolding and came out like a mother bear to protect her cubs. Angry and vulgar words were shouted by both parties. Nothing was settled other than going back to their respective homes. A quiet coldness descended on the relationship between the neighbors and nothing more was said.

Court: Some months later Chris and Don received a summons to appear in court regarding a small claims. They were being sued several thousand dollars for damage to their neighbor's property. Just prior to going to the small claims hearing, the parties opted to try to mediate the case. The mediation started off contentiously with hollering, name calling etc. Finally the mediator, through various techniques and continuous guidance, calmed everyone down and motivated them to communicate in an inclusive way. The mediator urged them to figure out exactly what happened, and he would help them have the difficult conversation. They agreed to give it a try.

The following is a summary of two hours of mediation.

The young boys were fidgeting and enjoying themselves to such an extent I don't think they had any realization of what was going on around them. Yet, it was good that they were present. Their fidgeting and self-centered world revealed that they were just kids.

Balanced Communication: The arguing and yelling continued for some time until the parties settled down and started talking in normal tones.

Chris: "I'm sorry but I didn't know that your property line was just a 150' behind our house." **(Concept & Feelings)** "I thought it was about halfway between our two homes." **(Concept)** "I should have checked with you before assuming where the property line was." **(Humanness)**

Anne: "Well you should have known. I put a rock out there to mark it." **(Concept)**

Chris: "Again I'm sorry." **(Feelings & Humanness)** "I hope you'll accept my apology." **(Humanness)** "We just moved here recently and hope to eventually buy the place. My husband works at the local bank." **(Concepts)**

Anne: "You mean you're thinking of being regular neighbors and be part of the neighborhood?" **(Concept & Humanness)** "That's good to hear." **(Interest & Feelings)** "But we still have to settle on the damages done by your boys to our landscaping." **(Concept)** "I had a professional landscaper come in and preserve the natural setting while opening up the views and establishing natural paths. It cost us several thousand dollars and the boys just undid much of what I paid for. I got an estimate on returning things to a natural state and thus the request for $3,000." **(Concept)** Don't you think that's fair?" **(Humanness)**

Don: "Anne and I think that's a lot of money for a few rocks and plants being moved by our kids. We certainly can't afford to pay this amount and don't want a judgment appearing on our credit report. **(Concept)** The kids meant no harm. We were unaware of the closeness of the property line and we want to be good neighbors. **(Concept & Humanness)** We plan to be here a long time. **(Concept)** We love everything about this place. **(Feelings)** Isn't there some way we could work this out?" **(Interest & Humanness)**

Anne: "All my husband and I want is things to be back the way they were." **(Concept)** If you can do that Bob and I will be happy." **(Concept, Interest, Feelings & Humanness)**

Don: "I have a landscaper friend, who owes me something. Would you be acceptable to have him restore the landscaping to your satisfaction?" **(Concept & Humanness)**

Anne: "Yes! Let's set a date by which the job will be done and then let's agree to check the results out together. **(Concept & Humanness)** Bob and I would like you to come over for coffee in the meantime and bring the kids to try some of my homemade cookies." **(Concept, Interests, Feelings & Humanness)**

Postscript: An agreement was written up that was accepted by the court, the kids found proxy grandparents and lines of communication were opened between neighbors.

Note: In the above examples, I interpreted the use of I, rather than the use of you (pointing fingers), as **Humanness**.

My perception is that the claim for $3,000 far exceeded the possible damages. The $3000 reflected the feelings of a personal violation of a bucolic setting that had been enjoyed for years and was desecrated by a family that was unknown. Once the new neighbors were seen as people with similar goals, the doors to resolution opened and the first steps to a good relationship were born. This is very common in mediation. Positions are often hard and demanding based on feelings and emotions, not necessarily facts. Once inclusive communication began and interests came forward both parties realized they had much in common. Creating a relationship became more important than the $3,000. If the case had gone to a small claims hearing, my guess is, the older couple would have been awarded much less money and the conversation needed for healing would not have taken place.

To listen dimensionally you have to listen with your mind and your heart. —C. Young

CHAPTER SEVEN

HELPS FOR RESOLUTION

Most inclusive communication will not require the use of the following. They're mentioned to assure good resources if needed.

If you can't resolve a topic during a conversation then give some thought to the following.

BRAINSTORMING

Brainstorming is just throwing out ideas as they come to mind. It is non-judgmental and seeks the best ideas no matter the source. Among any group of people, there are all kinds of ideas floating around. Brainstorming is a good non-threatening way to allow each person to think out loud, out of the box, while having some fun. The fun aspect of brainstorming gets things going. Negativity cuts off creative thinking.

Once all the ideas are out, they are evaluated and discussed. Ideas may be shared that people don't even like. My experience has been that sometimes these "crazy" ideas lead to better ideas. Participants need to feel free to share whatever comes to mind.

During a small claims mediation, while we were brainstorming, one person said, "Why don't you just write out a check for a $100,000 for me?" Everyone got laughing and they had a resolution within ten minutes.

Some guides for brainstorming:

1. Turn it into a fun activity. Let the wildest ideas come out. They open doors to other practical ideas. Developing a fun positive experience opens peoples' minds. Psychologically speaking we're opening the intellectual side of our brain to the creative artistic side.
2. Encourage random participation with no coercion. The greatest ideas often come from the least likely sources.
3. Don't evaluate any idea until there is a consensus that there are enough ideas on the table.
4. Gather the ideas into categories. Note: Many brainstorms falter at this step, resulting in little or no action.
5. Prioritize the categories and select the ideas that are possible.
6. Pick those you would like to discuss further and possibly implement.
7. Develop a consensus on those to be implemented and the means to do so.

TRUE FRIENDS

True friends will tell us the truth and not what we want to hear. They are persons of integrity and are concerned for our welfare. True friends can explain why they think we are right or wrong. We can trust them to tell us what's best for us in a situation and because we trust them, we give their ideas serious thought. Telling the truth, accepting accountability and responsibility, and being reliable are all part of the package of true friendship. Conversations with true friends are usually inclusive, openly empathetic and efforts are made to understand each other's perceptions. True friends include relatives, teachers, counselors, pastors, law enforcement, employers, etc.

"We need people in our lives with whom we can be as open as possible. To have real conversations with people may seem like such a simple, obvious suggestion, but it involves courage and risk."

—St. Thomas Moore

TRUE RESEARCH

True research goes to the best source for obtaining information. It gives us the facts, or at least shares with us that this is just an opinion or theory. Simply because we read or hear something or look it up on the internet doesn't necessarily mean it's true. True research goes deeper than that. Most true research goes to the original documents on a subject or documents that refer to the original documents. Sometimes, we may be able to talk directly to the person working on a research project. From my experience, listening to short five minute explanations of complex situations has never given me a full understanding or appreciation of them.

Some observations regarding research:

1. It takes effort and time to ascertain facts, especially facts that carry the baggage of many opinions.
2. In dealing with translations of accounts, the difficulty of ascertaining facts is compounded.
3. Conclusions from various facts must be based on a logical process.
4. Facts often become clouded through the lenses of perception.
5. Understanding how formulas support facts can be difficult.
6. Inclusive communication is a must during a controversy over "facts".

RECREATING A TRUST THAT HAS BEEN LOST

This is a repetition of an earlier concept. I repeat it due to its important role in life. Remember, lack of trust stands in the way of inclusive communication and resolutions.

Recreating lost trust is a step by step process that is not only tedious but at times discouraging. It takes patience and complete openness. Small steps are better than large ones. A leap in trust can create a chasm of mistrust if there is a problem. A small step may mean a small slide backwards but not to the bottom of a chasm. Slow small steps to recreate a lost trust, is a better way to go. Trust is earned. This takes time. It takes much inclusive communication.

The trust question, **"What can I do to earn or earn back your trust?"** is one way to allow another person to know that you're willing to do whatever it takes to have a trust relationship. This simple sentence can be difficult to say and even more difficult to respond to.

An observation on trust:

1. Picture in your mind a staircase. You take one step at a time.
2. Imagine making a leap when you can't quite see where you are going to land.
3. Trust is fragile. Take the steps rather than the leap.

COURTEOUS CURIOSITY-PSYCHOLOGISTS CALL IT APPRECIATIVE INQUIRY

This is particularly effective in dialoguing with people of a different culture, educational background or interests. We are in an unfamiliar environment and need to accept this. We inquire because we are truly interested for our own growth.

> While visiting my brother-in-law on a Native American reservation in southwest USA, I went into the trading post to buy some film. Unable to find it, I asked the clerk where the film

was. I asked three times and each time she glanced away. Finally she said that it was over there. I left the trading post and told my brother-in-law what had happened. He broke out laughing. She had told me three times and I hadn't known it. In their culture the people point with their nose. On reflection, the clerk had glanced, (pointed with her nose three times) to let me know where the film was, but I got frustrated rather than being thankful for her telling me right away where the film was. Remember, I was a visitor in their home and should have been sensitive to their way of doing things.

Accepting something that is strange to us can be difficult. To admit we might benefit from it can be a personal challenge. To accept that we can grow from the experience becomes a positive mind opening experience. A key element in inclusive communication.

"Be curious, not judgmental."

—Walt Whitman

CHAPTER EIGHT

THE BLOCK GAME

The block game, which is explained below, is an enjoyable way to practice inclusive communication. It's a perfectly enjoyable way for families and small groups to learn communication skills. It's non-threatening. Components of the game are easy to make or buy. I've seen people get so good at the game that it looks like they are reading each other's mind. As I evaluated these experiences, it became evident that their communication was inclusive and the non- verbal played an important role. In family situations where more inclusive communication is needed between siblings, this game can be very helpful.

The truly constructive piece about the block game is the **Interest. "We want us to succeed."**

PARTS NECESSSARY FOR THE BLOCK GAME

The parts necessary for the block game are simple. There are two identical sets of blocks. Each set has between 6 and 10 blocks. None of the blocks within each set are identical. There may be squares, rectangles, triangles etc. of different sizes. Thus each set will be identical but within each set there will be different shapes and sizes of blocks. The other requirement is a screen that will be set on a table between the two sets of blocks. For a screen I use a cardboard box approximately 2 ½ feet square and 5 inches deep so that I can set it on end. Though not necessary, I print on both sides of the box some tools of inclusive communication. Thus the titles of paraphrasing, open ended questions, clarifying, summarizing and empathizing face the players during the game.

INSTRUCTIONS FOR THE GAME

Two people sit at a table with a screen separating them so that they cannot see each other. In front of each person is the set of blocks. The screen also prevents each person from seeing the blocks of the other person.

The first player arranges his blocks in any way he wants. Once the blocks are arranged by the first player, he explains to the second player how to arrange his blocks so that they agree with his arrangement. The second player arranges his blocks as instructed while also clarifying etc. to assure his perceptions agree with the first player. This use of inclusive communication tools switches back and forth as the players verify that their concepts are in synch. Thus, the players arrange the blocks using the behavioral skills and tools of inclusive communication and end only when they agree that their arrangements are identical, even though they can't see each other's arrangement. It's similar to not being comfortable about another's perceptions until we verify them and feel that we understand and feel understood. Interestingly, empathy often plays a major role in arranging the blocks correctly.

The participants often want to end too soon. The mentor can encourage the second person to paraphrase on how his blocks are arranged. Often this results in a minor correction and more clarification until the arrangements are identical. This emphasizes not to assume and to clarify and verify.

Within a family or group of associates, I encourage something like a cheer leading squad. They encourage the use of the behaviors and tools of constructive communication without giving away verbally or non-verbally whether or not the two arrangements are close to being identical. Thus the onlookers (cheerleaders) become positive inputs for the use of the behaviors and tools and positive reinforcements.

I can't emphasize enough that many teams want to end too soon without a final paraphrase.

When I'm mentoring my seminar on Inclusive Communication, I refer to Learning Opportunities (LOs). When either or both of the participants in the block game are not getting their perceptions across, I call a time out for an LO. Almost always the difficulty exists with the failure to use one or more of the skills or behaviors mentioned in this guide. This has been more humbling to me than to the participants. The struggle to remove the past paradigms of communication seems to be a lifetime effort. LOs are **always** expressed in a positive way, i.e., suggestions, other alternatives etc.

Once the parties agree that they have done everything to arrange the blocks in the same way, then remove the screen and talk constructively about what happened. Let the participants take the lead. Their comments are often very insightful about what happened and what happened to them.

OTHER OPTIONS FOR THE BLOCK GAME

Have a player **in role** say nothing or just yes or no. Thus the person giving instructions may have NO idea whether or not the other person is cooperating. He just hears yes or no or nothing. This can be a powerful way of bringing out the advantages of constructive communication. Use this positively.

Lack of dialogue can become a real learning opportunity. Make sure the role player understands and accepts he is role playing. To emphasize this, assign the role player a temporary name. This is important and frees up the role player to play the role. It is thus clear that his actions and words do NOT reflect who he is. In certain situations it may be best to have each person be themselves.

I've used the block game hundreds of times and in some very difficult training situations. It has always been fun, rewarding and instructional.

CHAPTER NINE

VISUALS

ANOTHER VISUAL FOR CHAPTER FIVE THAT BRINGS OUT THE CONFUSION THAT IS OFTEN PRESENT

Communication can be faulty if we don't identify the feelings/emotions that come from our needs and expectations, so that we can handle them properly.
Observation
Idea – Thought

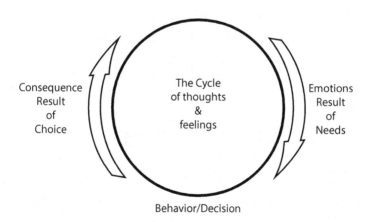

Behavior/Decision

My dad used to say,
"It's better to try and fail than not try."

PART TWO

CHAPTER ONE

THE PATH FOR CHALLENGING SITUATIONS

Part Two explains a mentored path that is used in contentious situations. This chapter provides a flow chart of the complete path.

The Path consists of an **Opening Statement, Story Telling, Understanding, Topics, Options** and **Solutions**. The path is designed to maximize participation and minimize obstructions. The participants' symbols are different as are their perceptions. The mentor is co-partial in the middle. He is neither a rectangle nor an oval. The arrows indicate the flow of information.

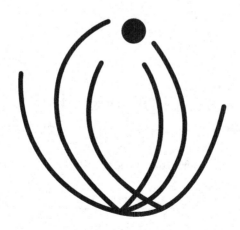

The seed of understanding

Opening Statement

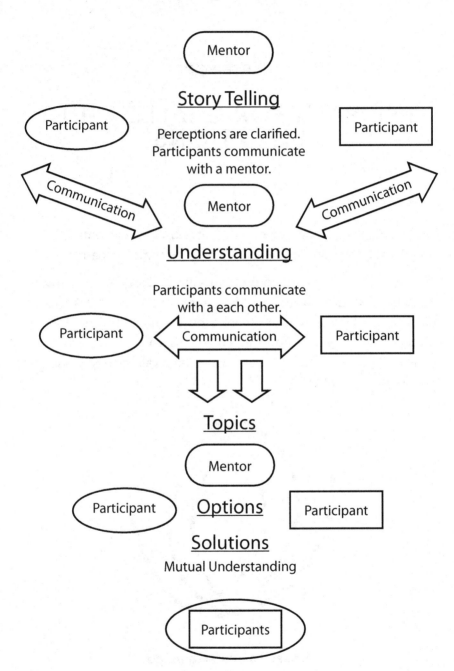

CONSTRUCTIVE COMMUNICATION

Brief explanation of the flow charts' topics and symbols.

The Opening Statement by the mentor sets the tone for the Path.

The Oval and Rectangle represent the participants who see things differently.

The Location of the Ovals and Rectangles change as the participants get closer to understanding.

The Rounded Corner Rectangle represents the mentor who is co-partial. He assures the participants equality of presence.

Arrows define the flow of information.

Story Telling is the initial communication by the participants with the mentor.

Understanding - The participants communicate with each other. During this time, the mentor is more of an observer who helps inclusive communication proceed.

Down Arrows indicate the gathering of topics by the mentor.

Topics are identified by the mentor during understanding. This gathering is identified by the down arrows.

Options are the result of brainstorming by the participants.

Solution(s) are the result of choosing the viable options and agreeing on how to implement them.

In actual practice, as the path unfolds, it may bounce back and forth among **Understanding, Story Telling, Options and Solutions**. Mentors trust the path. It is the compass that leads to solutions. The path should not hinder the development of understanding and resolution. Participants need to feel they understand and they need to feel understood themselves.

Picture in your mind how parents, teachers, coaches, pastors, supervisors, etc. could apply this process to find a path to common understandings, healings and agreement.

The path's guidelines can be adapted to fit most situations. The path exemplifies reaching solutions through inclusive communication. The reasons why it works will be explained in the following chapters.

The path leads through a forest. We never know and don't try to know the beauty to which it will lead.

Variations of the path are used by professional mediators. They are trained extensively in the skills used to facilitate difficult conversations that arise during complex mediations.

The next chapters explain why each step contributes to the success of the path. Within each chapter there will be a continuing scenario exemplifying that part of the path.

CHAPTER TWO

THE OPENING STATEMENT

The "Opening Statement" sets the tone, explains the path and its boundaries and introduces the mentor and his persona. The scenario for this chapter will exemplify an informal "Opening Statement".

The mentor explains and amplifies the following in the "Opening Statement".

The mentor introduces himself, welcomes the participants and thanks them for giving the path a try. He then obtains the names of the participants and assures this is the way they wish to be addressed. This creates a relationship of I want to work with you, and that I want to address you properly. This may seem trivial but over the years I've found it's beneficial. Small steps with personal input help break the ice and create relationships. All of the above helps the mentor adjust to the participants' needs.

The mentor assures the participants that the room and the next hour or so have been set aside to have a meaningful conversation without interruptions. The message is that this is important, and I want the time and privacy you might need for success. The question of confidentiality will be dictated by the circumstances and the desires of the participants. This can be seen by the participants as a personal recognition and structural component for lasting solutions. In a professional mediation a confidentiality agreement is usually signed by all present.

The mentor explains that the path is voluntary and can be ended at any time if a participant so wishes. This creates a buy-in on the part of the participants. By not leaving, the message is that they want to work toward a resolution. An additional message is that each has a point to share. In less formal situations the mentor might ask the participants to agree not to walk away during the process. This assures a commitment to the path and a complete hearing. Most people want to be heard. In parental situations confidentiality will probably not be mentioned.

The mentor explains that participants, before agreeing to anything, can get professional or parental advice. In certain situations this calms participants who are afraid to proceed. In less formal situations this probably will not be mentioned. In professional situations mediators may not give legal advice.

In conjunction with the above, the mentor makes clear that he simply helps the participants have a difficult conversation and will not suggest how to resolve the situation. The mentor should not get involved in evaluating evidence such as photos, contracts etc. The participants need to explain these items to each other. A mentor isn't making decisions or judgements and should not be perceived as doing so. He is simply assisting a difficult conversation. This empowers the participants. Some participants resist accepting this responsibility.

The mentor emphasizes that the participants are there to resolve a situation not attack personalities. This keeps personal attacks to a minimum which opens minds to the situation and not personalities.

The mentor stresses that good faith is a key to a resolution. The participant should put his efforts into trying to understand the other person's perceptions. Participants often get caught up in defense or attack rather than understanding. My experience is that when good faith is present in both of the parties, a resolution and healing take place most of the time.

The mentor explains that a caucus is a private meeting. He might wish to meet with each participant privately for various reasons. If there are several participants involved on one side of a topic, they might wish to meet privately to agree on something before proceeding. This reassures the participants who may feel very alone. If the mentor senses a participant feels left out, he may reassure him through a caucus.

It is the responsibility of the mentor to see that the participants are informed and feel part of the path.

The mentor then explains the steps of the path. The participants know what to expect. They have a path.

He ends with, "If there are any questions feel free to ask them at any time". This assures the participants that the mentor is there to help.

In the case of a parent as mentor, he may have to struggle to get into the persona of a mentor.

The mentor sets the tone in the opening statement, so let's use a scenario to exemplify the path. The same scenario will continue through all the chapters.

A SCENARIO FOR OPENING STATEMENT

Background: Dad finds two of his sons arguing over whose turn it is to take the garbage to the landfill. The mom is just sick and tired of the constant bickering and it's getting to her.

Characters: Dad; 17 year old son – John; 16 year old son – Paul; Mom.

SCENARIO

Dad – "You two boys and I need to sit down and find a way to end this pettiness. Let's go into my den where we'll have some privacy and talk this over. We can talk this out as men without any silly distractions. Do you have time now and can you guarantee that there won't be any interruptions?"

Boys – "We agree and we have the time."

Dad – "I'm certainly proud of you boys for giving it a try. You know how the path works. Each of you will have the chance to explain your perception of the situation to me. Once I think I understand your perceptions

I hope you start to talk directly with each other, and I'll listen and see what needs to be worked out. Once we have an idea of what needs to be changed, you'll brainstorm and I might throw in a few ideas. Boy! I hope you have some good ideas. I'm tired of all the bickering. Then from the brainstorms, you'll start to work out a possible resolution. Let's agree not to leave the den until we have this mess all worked out. Your mom is fit to be tied and I don't blame her. I think we can share our decisions with the rest of the family. Are we in agreement to all of this?"

Boys – "Yes."

Dad – "Do you have any questions? Okay, who wants to start in giving me his perception of the situation?"

NOTES ON THE SCENARIO

Getting the "Yes" and "agree" replies from the boys **sets a positive tone.**

Referring to the discussion as men's talk and no silly distractions, **gives a strong recognition** of the boys being able to act as men. The "without any silly distractions" enters a bit of levity which often softens things up dramatically.

The Dad's "when I think I understand the perceptions" **sends a message of humanness.**

Dad's "Boy! I hope you have some good ideas" **offers a challenge** with fun attached.

Reference to the path indicates the boys know it, and it has most likely been helpful in the past.

"Any questions," **demonstrates** to the boys, that dad is there to help.

Giving the boys a choice of who starts initiates decision making.

Dad uses neutral terms such as situation in place of problem and what needs to be changed rather than what mistakes need to be addressed. This maintains neutrality and avoids misperceptions. A simple negative term can trigger strong emotions in some people.

Dad may have slipped up by using the word mess (a negative term), but non-verbally (the way he said it) could have lightened things up. **A good move.**

This "Opening Statement" took a few minutes, but **sets the tone and boundaries** to reach a solution. There's no yelling, no cajoling. It's just this is the way we, as a family, resolve our differences. This is very positive. It is important to remember that each mentor will have his own style for the "Opening Statement".

SUMMARY

The opening statement assures equal and complete hearings, provides a safe and comfortable setting, provides a known structure, exemplifies good communication, assures that all substantive issues are covered and feelings and procedural issues are addressed.

CHAPTER THREE

STORY TELLING

During "Story Telling" the participants talk directly with the mentor.

The mentor exemplifies the use of inclusive communication skills.

The mentor demonstrates the value of good faith.

The mentor reassures. He validates, empathizes, clarifies and summarizes during "Story Telling".

The mentor addresses emotions through empathy and questioning. It's called going to the heat. Done well and empathetically it can be effective.

The mentor guarantees that each participant is heard without serious interruptions.

Each participant has a chance to explain his perception of the situation to the mentor who assures a clear understanding of the participants' perception. As a mentor, I use the term perception frequently. This has proven successful through the years. Participants often refer to it later as being an important concept.

The participants are telling their story to a mentor who simply wants to understand and has no ax to grind. Wanting to understand is exemplified by the mentor's use of the good faith practices of clarifying, paraphrasing etc. A mentor never assumes he understands a perception.

In many cases this will be the first time a participant will have fully heard the other person's perception.

Much of the emotional part that would have existed in direct participant communication is removed because explanations are shared with the mentor.

The participants get to feel empowered and being heard.

Most importantly the participants start to feel they understand, and even more importantly, feel that they are being understood.

Often the participants slip into the next step of "Understanding" without any urging. Having heard each other's perception, as explained to the mentor, they're wanting to really clear the air without the fog of emotions and foul language.

SCENARIO FOR STORY TELLING.

Dad – "Who would like to start and share his perception of the situation?"

John – "Since I'm the older of us I would like to explain why I'm right."

Dad – "We're not judging anything now. We're just getting each of your perceptions of the situation."

John – "Okay! Paul and I take turns taking the rubbish to the dump on Saturdays. It was my turn last week, but it snowed so hard that I couldn't get to the dump. Now, Paul wants me to go to the dump with two week's load of garbage and this week it's Paul's turn to go. It's as simple as that. Paul just doesn't want to fulfill his responsibility. I'm ready to go next week. I plan ahead so that when I go to the dump there aren't any conflicts. Paul's got to grow up and do some planning. End of story."

Dad – "So my understanding is that you and Paul alternate Saturdays for taking the garbage to the dump, and last Saturday you couldn't go due to the snow. Now, you think Paul is responsible for taking this week's rubbish, which includes all that packing from our new appliances, and last week's garbage to the dump. Is that correct?

John – "Not quite dad. I plan ahead and so the Saturdays I go to the dump are important. I set them aside from other commitments. So this Saturday I have another commitment. I'm meeting my friends to play basketball."

Dad – "Is there anything you want to add before Paul explains his perception of the situation?"

John – "No! Paul knows it's his turn to take the garbage to the dump."

Dad – "Paul, what is your perception of the situation?"

Paul – "Dad, I don't think it's fair that John skips a week, creates a double load for me and then wants me to go out alone to the dump with the rubbish. The least he can do is go out with me this week to help. Last week was his turn and he didn't take care of the rubbish. Now he wants me to take his load and mine to the dump. He keeps insisting about going out next week and that this week it's my turn. By the way, I do plan ahead, but I can't plan for snow storms and I'm old enough to adjust my schedule to mother-nature. It sounds like John hasn't grown up enough."

John – "There you go again, baby brother. Next week is my turn and I'll gladly go to the dump."

Paul – "I didn't know any particular Saturday was important to you."

John – "There's a lot you don't know."

Dad – "Remember, we're here to understand and in order to do so we need to try not to insult or argue, but to find out what the other person's perceptions are. So let's start communicating and not just talking. What I hear you saying, is that you don't feel it's fair to have to take a double load out alone this Saturday and that you do plan ahead but can't plan for the unknown. Is that correct?"

Paul – "That's about it and I don't like to be called baby brother?"

John – "Despite everything I think Paul and I have a pretty good picture of things, so I'm just going to be the big brother and ask Paul some questions."

Paul – "Ask what you want and we'll work something out to keep Mom happy, just as long as I don't have to go to the dump alone today."

Dad – "Remember, that while you're talking things over, I'm going to write down the topics about which we need to brainstorm for working out something to which we can all agree."

NOTES ON THE SCENARIO

The dad **gave the boys a choice** of who would start.

The dad made it clear that there was **no judging** at this time.

The dad **paraphrased** John and John in turn **clarified** some of dad's paraphrasing.

Clarification of the mentor's paraphrasing is fairly common.

The dad also paraphrased Paul.

Each of the boys is adamant about his position.

Paul's, "Ask what you want and we'll work something out" **is a conciliatory gesture**. It was an opportunity for amplification, but dad missed it.

Though the brothers didn't exactly follow telling their story one at a time, the dad recognized the true picture was coming out and opted not to interfere. In very contentious situations, allowing only one participant at a time to give a brief synopsis of his story without any interruptions goes a long way. This becomes obvious in demanding situations.

Dad wisely ignored, John's judgmental statement, "Paul knows it's his turn."

The true interests behind the positions are not clear.

The boys accept that they understand the other's perceptions.

More importantly the boys feel understood.

The boys in this case initiate the next step of "Understanding".

During "Understanding" they'll be talking to each other.

The dad will write down the topics that will come up in "Understanding". This encourages the participants to cover all the bases.

SUMMARY

1. **Avoids** a direct confrontation between the participants.
2. The mentor **exemplifies** good faith, i.e., listens to understand rather than to figure out how to answer.
3. The mentor **reiterates perceptions** which are often clarified by the participant.
4. It **opens up the possibility** of new information to the other participant.
5. It gives the participants **the feeling of being heard** and, more importantly, **the feeling of being understood**.
6. It gives the participants **the opportunity to blow off steam** in a controlled environment.
7. Mentor **assures crystal clear articulation** of the perceptions.
8. Possibly for the first time, the participants **hear completely** the perceptions of the other participant.
9. The success of the next step, "Understanding", is normally dependent on the success of "Story Telling".
10. The mentor and "Story Telling" are normally not necessary when people can communicate inclusively. It's when emotions, strong positions, etc. get in the way that we use a path.
11. A mentor should **never** assume that a perception is understood. By not assuming that he understands, he **sends a message of wanting clarity**.

CHAPTER FOUR

UNDERSTANDING

During "Understanding" the participants talk directly with each other. The mentor may give guidance or assistance. Usually he slips into the background and identifies the topics that need to be addressed while the participants converse.

"Understanding" offers the following for success.

The participants can expand on the perceptions shared during "Story Telling" and work to understand the interests behind them.

The mentor can assist as the participants open up and start being more human, a catalyst for solutions.

The participants, by talking directly to each other, add the dimension of non-verbal by reaching out directly to each other and uncovering their relationship.

Acknowledging a relationship opens the door for give and take for solutions.

The mentor becomes more a supporter than a mentor. The message is that this is their time and their energies build on themselves. What has been negative starts turning to the positive.

During "Understanding", a mentor usually recognizes that there will be a resolution. Often this happens long before the participants realize it, and he can encourage the participants to continue when they get disheartened.

The time spent during "Understanding" often turns into an ally by creating the insight that we need to move on with our lives in a positive way. This is a significant advance in the resolution process.

Occasionally participants can't explain their perceptions during "Understanding". The mentor has to assist them.

A SCENARIO FOR UNDERSTANDING

John – "I don't get it. It's your turn to take the rubbish to the dump and you won't do it. Since its two weeks of rubbish, I'm even willing to help you load it in the truck. On top of that, since it's a big load, you'll get to drive our new crew-cab pickup. What a deal. I just want to get back to my schedule of going out on the 2nd and 4th Saturday of the month, and you want to screw it up."

Paul – "What's the big deal about the 2nd and 4th Saturday of the month? We've always alternated Saturdays on going to the dump and when there's a 5th Saturday we flip a coin. So maybe we need to flip a coin for today.

John – "No way! I'm sticking to my 2nd and 4th Saturday of the month and no one is going to change that. It's special."

Paul – "Special! What's so special about going to the dump?" If it's so special, why don't you take the rubbish out every Saturday?"

Dad – "Okay guys were not getting anywhere and you're starting to holler at each other. John, what's special about the 2nd and 4th Saturdays of the month?"

John – "That's when Alice is in charge of the weigh in."

Dad – "Who's Alice?'

Paul – "She's Ramon's daughter. They sit a few pews in front of us on Sunday."

Dad – "John, what do you know about her?"

John – "Very little. But I sure want her to be my friend."

CONSTRUCTIVE COMMUNICATION

Dad – "So that's why the 2nd and 4th Saturdays are so important to go to the dump."

John – "I would go every Saturday if she was on duty at the weigh in. Last time she even asked my name. It would be nice to visit with her on Sunday. You and mom could get to know her too."

Paul – "Now I know why the 2nd and 4th Saturdays are so important. So you owe me one if I decide to take the rubbish today. My guess is that you don't want Alice to meet your good looking younger brother."

John – "No chance she'd ever ask for your name. Anyway you already have Nancy."

Paul – "Okay, you win this round, but I'm still not going to the dump today."

John – "Why not? I'll help you load and when you get to the dump they help you unload. In the meantime I can meet the guys for a pickup game of basketball, and next Saturday I'll get to talk to Alice. Deal?"

Paul – "Will the rubbish fit in the back of the SUV?"

John – "No."

Paul – "Then no deal."

John – "What's going on? You couldn't ask for a sweeter deal."

Paul – "I'm not comfortable driving the new pickup to the dump. Dad always says, It's better to be safe than sorry. So, don't push me. This is a big deal and it's not because I'm your little brother."

Dad – "You're right there."

John – "So where do we go from here?"

Dad – "I think I've written down all the topics we need to discuss. Shall we brainstorm to see if we can work out something we can all live with?"

Boys – "This better be good."

NOTES ON THE SCENARIO

As the boys start to share ideas, it becomes apparent that there **are interests** behind their actions. It's the **"why"** to what they are doing.

The dad went to the heat. He picked up the non-verbal on why John was so emotional about the 2nd and 4th Saturdays.

These interests are gradually **explored and evaluated**. It's determined that they are very important to both boys.

The dad pushes to move on to brainstorming. He thinks he has all the pertinent topics and will verify this with the boys. It may turn out that during brainstorming they might have to go back to "Story Telling" or "Understanding".

SUMMARY

1. As the participants share concepts they start clarifying with each other.
2. More feelings are expressed and interests come out.
3. When a mentor goes to the heat the reasons behind strong feelings are uncovered and possibilities for resolution arise.

The seed of understanding

CHAPTER FIVE

BRAINSTORMING

From the topics Identified by the mentor during "Understanding", the brainstorming process produces options. Out of the options solutions are developed.

The options are the participants'. They create them which empowers them.

The participants categorize and prioritize the options.

The options create the roots for a solution.

Brainstorming gets the creative juices going and pushes the envelope of possibilities.

During brainstorming, insights are often created. Concepts come together in a way that the insight just seems to happen. The relaxed atmosphere of brainstorming allows the intellectual side of the brain to become receptive to the artistic side. A good example of an insight is whiteness. We see things that are white but whiteness itself is abstract, a result of an insight.

A SCENARIO FOR OPTIONS

Dad – "I think I have written down all the topics you mentioned that we need to address with brainstorming. Let me know if I've left out anything. Assignment of Saturdays to go to the dump, Alice, and driving the new pickup. Are there any others?

Paul – "I would like to put Mom on the list. After all she's been really flustered over all the bickering."

John – "I don't think we need Alice on the list. If we settle on Saturday assignment dates it will take care of this."

Dad – "If we take Alice off of the list, Mom and I still need to talk about her with you, John. We talked to Paul about Nancy."

John – "I agree Dad, but first I have to get to know her."

Dad – "So we need to agree on a schedule for going to the dump, driving the new pickup and mom's welfare? Which topic would you like to discuss first?"

Paul – "I would like to talk about Mom first, but maybe we should start with the Saturday schedule."

John – "I think we should combine driving the pickup and the Saturday schedule."

Dad – "That's okay with me. What do you think, Paul?"

Paul – "I would like to get this over with so whoever gets chosen to go to the dump can do it before lunch. I'm willing to combine the two and then Mom."

John – "I agree."

Dad – "Well let's get started with the brainstorming."

Paul – "Before we get started, I'd like us to agree that we don't blabber about our brainstorming. Some of things I might share I wouldn't want my friends to know about. Is that okay with you two?"

Dad & John – "Yes."

Dad – "Let's get started."

Paul – "I would like Dad to spend some time with me in getting me comfortable with the new pickup. I'm really scared driving that big diesel rig."

John – "I'd like to go along to observe when Dad works with Paul. I'll admit there are some things I need to get to know."

Paul – "We need to get to know how to properly tie down large loads in the pickup."

John – "We need to get to know how to change tires and put chains on the pickup, and what do we do if there is an accident."

Dad – "Boy, so far the brainstorming is simply putting me on the spot. But it's good to get all this out. Is there anything else you want to add regarding driving the pickup?"

Paul – "Yes! Who's responsible for keeping the pickup filled with diesel?"

John – "Okay, so who's responsible to make sure the tires are the right pressure and the engine has oil?"

Dad – "We can skip those two. I'll take on that responsibility."

Both boys – "Thanks Dad. We'll drop those two from the brainstorming"

Dad – "How about the Saturday scheduling?"

John – "We set it up so that I go to the dump on the 2nd and 4th Saturday of the month as long as Alice is covering that shift."

Paul – "When there's a load big enough that we need to take the pickup, both of us should go to the dump."

John – "Dad should go to the dump when it's Paul's turn and he needs to use the pickup."

Paul – "Dad could take a turn going to the dump."

John – "Maybe we should buy a new small pickup."

John – "We could pay the monthly fee for the city to pick up our rubbish."

Paul – "We could burn most of our garbage so we don't need to go to the dump every week."

Dad – "I think we have enough options on going to the dump on Saturday. What do you guys think?"

Paul – "If we think of another, we can still bring it up, can't we?"

Dad – "Sure."

Boys – "Let's go to the next topic."

Dad – "So what ideas do you have about Mom and her being upset over the arguing?"

John – "Buy a dozen roses."

Paul – "Take Mom out to dinner and tell her we're sorry and thank her for all she does."

John – "Both Paul and I are to blame, we should do something special together for Mom."

Dad – "Are there any other ideas regarding Mom?"

Boys - "Not for now."

Dad – "Okay, I've written a list of all the ideas. Now let's agree on how we can work together."

Paul – "Maybe it's too late, but I would like to add one more topic. How are we going to end our bickering?"

Dad – "Wow! That's a big one."

Boys together – "Let's do it."

Dad – "Okay, I'll add it to the list, but let's brainstorm on it after we've reached an agreement on the two topics we have on the table."

Boys together – "Let's get started."

NOTES ON THE SCENARIO

Dad **assures** that the boys have a buy-in on the topics to be discussed and **empowers them** by asking if there are any he missed or might be dropped.

Dad just **lets the boys run** with the brainstorming. To inhibit it would remove creativity.

Boys' response demonstrates that they feel **empowered.**

Boys throw out some out-of-the-box ideas. They're **comfortable brainstorming.**

"Let's do it" sends a strong message that the boys are **getting emotionally involved.**

"Let's get started" reiterates the boys **want to develop a path** to avoid bickering.

SUMMARY

1. The options and their prioritization are the participants'. They have bought into them.
2. The time spent brainstorming opens things up. It creates an energy.
3. The brainstorming of the participants creates the roots for the solutions.
4. Once rooted the solutions are theirs and they become committed to it.

CHAPTER SIX

SOLUTIONS

"Solutions" are the result of "Options" and "Brainstorming". The participants develop them. Often the mentor, because of past experience, can offer some wise assistance. In some situations the options are written on a board for all to see.

The Path enhances the opportunity for success for the following reasons:

The solutions are worked out by the participants. They are working from what they have formulated.

The path has continually freed them up, empowered them, involved them in a positive way, freed up their creative capacities and avoided negative input through use of neutral terms and absence of criticism.

A third co-partial party assured the above and legitimized their input.

Because the resolution is theirs the chance that it will be implemented is excellent.

A SCENARIO FOR <u>SOLUTIONS</u> AND EVENTUAL <u>RESOLUTION</u>

Dad – "You guys have to decide about the dump schedule and driving the new pickup. My understanding is that you want to decide on explaining things to Mom later. Is that correct?"

Paul – "That's right, and I think getting a second pickup would solve the Saturday problem."

John – "That might sound good, but I'm entering college next year and a new pickup might affect the monies going into our college education fund. Is that correct Dad?"

Dad – "A new or used small pickup would set the college fund back. Next fall is going to come sooner than we think. But you boys have to resolve this in a way that suits both of you."

Paul – "I never thought of the college education fund. In the long run both of us really want to go to college, and there's only so much we can earn in the summer to help pay for it. So I'm for having the college education fund as a priority, thus no pickup."

John – "I have to agree. Both of us know what a good education means. The way I see it is if Dad could help both of us get comfortable driving the crew-cab pickup most of our problem would be solved. I'll admit that I'm also not comfortable driving it and could use some mentoring."

Paul – "Boy! That's news to me. Welcome aboard big brother. I really would like you to be able to see Alice on the 2nd and 4th Saturdays. I know how much Nancy means to me. But I really don't want to take the crew-cab pickup to the dump. Dad, is there a way you could help?"

Dad – "Guys you're impressing me. I'll tell you what I'm willing to do. If we can finish this up in the next half hour, I can ride shotgun for Paul today and start getting him comfortable with the crew-cab pickup. But John you'll have to help load so I can get back in time for an appointment. Then, when the whole family goes to church on Sunday, I'll ride shotgun for both of you until you really feel comfortable. The crew-cab is intimidating. Mom will like this too. By next week you can get back to your regular schedule. How's that sound?"

Paul - "Wow, Dad, that's more than generous."

John – "I'll ditto that. We all become winners. Thanks Dad."

Dad – "Well you left the biggest challenge to last, Mom."

John – "Mom's always there and we seem to forget her."

Paul – "I just got an idea and I hope you don't think it's dumb. What if we surprised Mom and we take her out to dinner as a family and make prior arrangements for the restaurant to bring out a cake reading. <u>The best Mom in the world</u>.

John – "Wow! I like that idea and during dinner we could share how much she means to us."

Dad – "I think you guys came up with great solutions. I couldn't be more proud of you. I'll feel better about you driving the crew-cab and I'll be ecstatic when we all tell Mom how much she means to us and that we love her. I'll also set everything up at our favorite restaurant. I'm going to tell them to make this something special."

Paul – "Dad, when we take Mom to dinner and she asks why. Can we say, 'Just because,' and then really let her know how much we love her."

Dad – "Boy! That's a great idea, I'll let Anne know. She'll love it."

John – "I agree, Sis is a freshman and we need to get her involved in our thanks."

Paul – "We have one more matter and that is ending our bickering."

John – "Can we agree to sit down like we did today, and most likely we won't even need Dad?"

Paul – "Let's do it"

High fives all around.

Dad – "With what we've accomplished, I think we can move on without formalizing what we've talked about."

Paul – "I think I can talk for both of us. We're ready to move on."

John – "We sure are."

Dad – "Thanks again boys. I'm proud that you're my sons."

NOTES ON THE SOLUTIONS

Notice that some topics got lost in the discussion. This is normal.

Interests play an important part, **e.**g., education fund & driving comfortably.

The boys seemed to be on a roll. This could be from the **freedom and energies** of the brainstorm.

Dad **kept the ball in the boys' court**. E.g., "My understanding is that you want … "

The idea of a new small pickup wasn't rejected by the dad. He kept **the boys empowered.**

The boys **decided on their own** to reject the idea of the small pickup. This develops the concept of the need for prioritizing.

Both boys want to go to college. Dropping the idea of the small pickup is **mutually beneficial.**

The path was an eye opener. The boys **became aware** that the education fund is part of the family budget and that Dad has their futures at heart.

The interests of both boys wanting to become comfortable with the crew-cab surfaced.

Dad's stepping in and offering to ride shotgun is an **offer** and was well accepted. He was reading the signs and spoke up. He read the signs correctly.

Awareness that Dad wants **what's best** for the boys became apparent.

The mutual love for Mom is moving and infectious.

Dad's praise of the boys working this out added to the boys' **positive self-images.**

The high fives sent **a strong non-verbal message** that we're a team.

In this case, conflict **became an opportunity** from which the family grew.

What started out with bickering over going to the dump **became a path** to bring the family closer together.

The conversation of the scenario was **inclusive**.

The conflict could have been ignored and become a hidden agenda. It would always be there but unspoken. The path revealed the wound and **let the light of humanness in**.

Twenty minutes or so spent on the path **comes back a hundredfold.**

Over time, inclusive constructive communication will replace the path.

SUMMARY

1. Solutions are theirs. Ideally each adjusts his position with a result of trust and harmony.

2. A third party doesn't create a solution. Third party solutions often leave both participants unhappy and often lacking trust and harmony.

3. The monkeys on the backs are gone and the participants can move on.

4. Empowerments born of the path are uplifting.

5. Solutions, though rational, usually go through an emotional non rational process.

Over the years, I've developed a checklist. When emotions and tensions are high, we tend to forget or rush, and that's the last thing we want to do. I purposely slow down at the beginning of the path. It tends to get others to slow down and start settling in. The use of a checklist keeps me on track and sends a message that this is important.

The following checklist is not as extensive as the one I use. It's a model from which each mentor should develop his own checklist. I use the term tickler for my checklist since its wording awakens concepts that I need to explain in the "Opening Statement".

I recommend the use of a checklist the first few times a mentor walks "The Path". I still faithfully use my checklist at all my mediations.

POSSIBLE CHECKLIST

1. Welcome & Congratulate
2. Introduce self and get names participants wish used
3. Confidentiality & determine how want applied
4. Mandatory reporter if applies
5. Voluntary/would like promise not to walk out
6. Good faith
7. Mentor simply facilitator
8. If would like outside input, say so.
9. Steps of "The Path"
10. Any questions

SOME FINAL OVERALL THOUGHTS

The scenario was written in the light of 20+ years of mediating experience. It embodies the belief of many of my peers that the need for mediation is usually the result of the lack of good communication. The longer this lack persists, the greater the difficulty in reaching resolutions. During family mediations, which are often very difficult, we often hear, "Do you remember." The participant is referring to an event that happened over 10 years ago and it has been festering ever since. "The Path" is a way to address issues in the present and let the light of humanness in.

It's better to address topics while they are fresh in our minds. They don't become hidden agendas or festering wounds. During "The Path" we attempt to use only neutral words.

"The Path", is an adaptation of a facilitative process many mediators use. My experience has been that when there is good faith on both sides, the participants come to a resolution most of the time. Note: I say, the participants were successful not the mediator was successful. Facilitative mediators simply help people have difficult conversations. It's the participants' conversation and **their** solutions.

As a mediator I wish more families etc. would use a path. It is proactive rather than reactive. Even better is a path without a mentor. This healthy dialogue is inclusive communication.

THE PATH OVERALL

1. Relationships are improved.
2. New information is uncovered.
3. There can be true healing of mind, body and heart.
4. Participants learn more about themselves and each other.
5. Lasting solutions can be created.
6. Better solutions are developed.
7. Empathetic values surface.

Before concluding I feel I should mention that my tendency is to read guides and think of how they fit other people. This side steps their purpose. I have to start with me. How do I apply this guide to me?

CAVEATS

Is inclusive communication always successful? The quick answer is no. From my 80+ years of life's experiences and over 1,500 formal mediations, I offer the following thoughts. These have not been scientifically researched.

Some people refuse to accept personal responsibility. They prefer to have others decide for them.

Some people can't imagine how people can have different perceptions of the same situation. Their perception has to be correct. So what is there to discuss?

Some people's emotions or prejudices so cloud their thinking that inclusive communication is impossible.

For those who want everything black and white, going to trial with a judge deciding the black or the white may be the way to go.

When humanness is lacking, inclusive communication is impossible.

In some of the above situations a resolution may be reached for a monetary settlement without inclusive communication, but healing is usually not part of the resolution.

In this guide I refer to a mentor facilitating "The Path". Professional mediators have intense and extensive training in all of the skills mentioned in this guide plus training in additional skills.

I believe in inclusive communication as a way to grow, learn, resolve differences and create relationships, but it is not suitable in all situations.

ABOUT THE AUTHOR

Charlie Young was ordained a Catholic priest in 1958. He served as a pastor, Director of a Diocesan Office of Religious Education and was a chaplain in the Naval Reserve during this time. He formed a team which developed and presented seminars on communication skills and the adult learning process. He obtained his Private Pilot's Certificate to facilitate travel. Charlie also spent 8 months as a pastor in a remote area of Chiapas, Mexico where his flying abilities were called into service.

Upon leaving the priesthood, Charlie functioned as a single and multi-engine instrument flight instructor with advanced and instrument ground training certificates and an Air Transport Pilot Certificate.

When offered, Charlie accepted an initial position in human resources and safety for an electrical contractor. This led to a sequence of further corporate opportunities and training. Prior to retirement he was the Head Total Quality Management Trainer for a large electrical contracting company.

Since retirement in 1997, Charlie has lived in Bend, OR and has been active as a volunteer in the mediation programs of Deschutes County Circuit Court, Redmond Justice Court and Community Solutions. Presently he assists in the training of mediators, has developed a <u>Constructive Communication</u> seminar and a short written corollary for the application of inclusive communication for companies. Upon request, Charlie professionally facilitates mediations.

charlie.y.bend@gmail.com

SOURCES THAT HAVE INFLUENCED THE CONCEPTS OF THIS BOOK

Conflict Resolution by Daniel Dana

Everything Belongs by Richard Rohr

Getting Past No by William Ury

Getting to Yes by Roger Fisher and William Ury

Getting Together by Roger Fisher and Scott Brown

Nonviolent Communication by Marshall B. Rosenberg

My many mediator friends

WHEN COMMUNICATING

Drive your **CAR.**

Be **C**ompassionate - Be **A**ccountable - Be **R**esponsible

CPSIA information can be obtained
at www.ICGtesting.com
Printed in the USA
FSOW04n0459131217
42115FS